Pioneer Settler

Enoch Harris
First African American settler in Kalamazoo County
1830

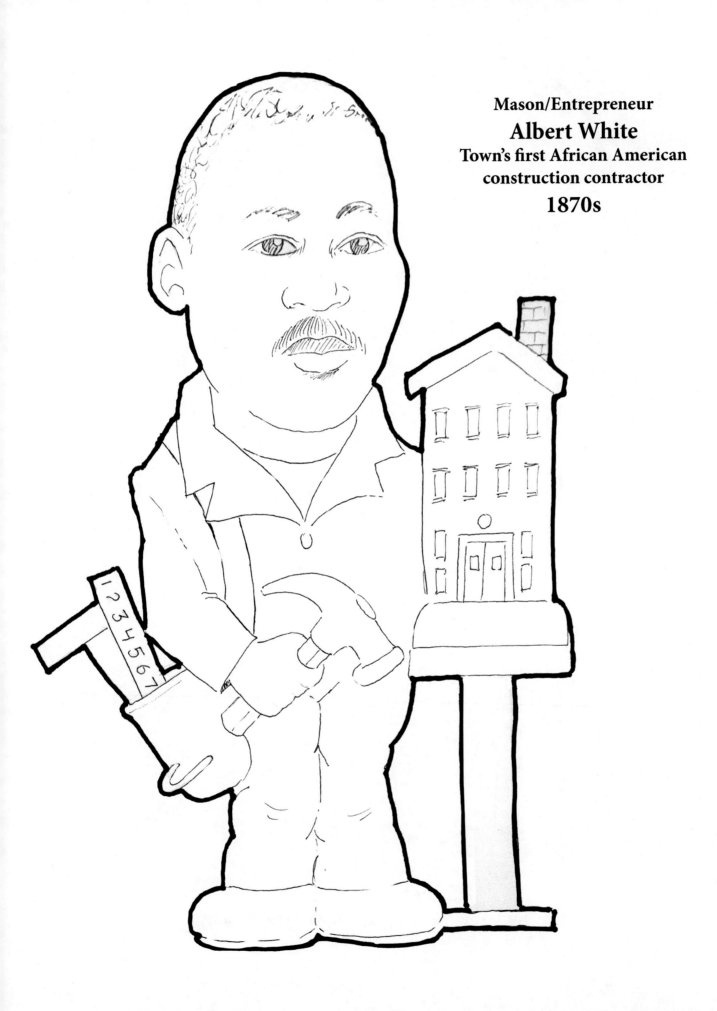

Mason/Entrepreneur
Albert White
Town's first African American
construction contractor
1870s

Mail Carrier
Frank White
**First African American to deliver
mail in Kalamazoo area**
1891

Politician
Wallace Stafford
Kalamazoo's first African American
justice of the peace
1894

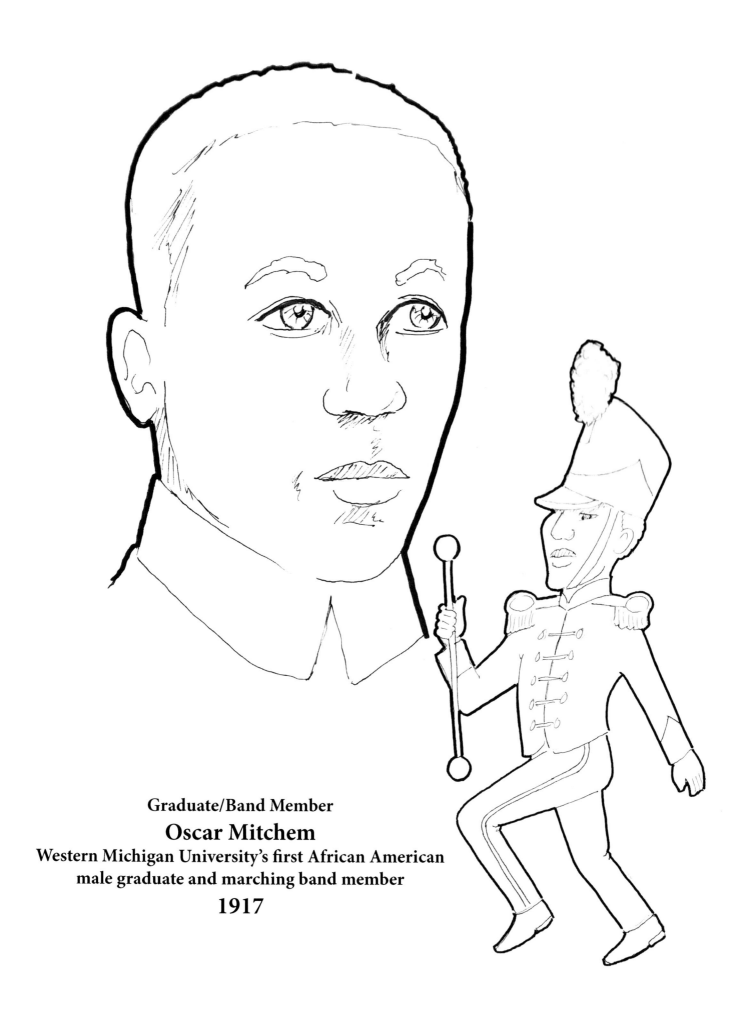

Graduate/Band Member
Oscar Mitchem
Western Michigan University's first African American
male graduate and marching band member
1917

Doctor
Dr. Cornelius Alexander
First African American doctor and surgeon in Kalamazoo
1931

Judge
Charles Pratt
Kalamazoo's first African American
attorney and judge
1935

Artist/Historian
Murphy Darden
Murphy and twin brother, Irvin, were the
first African American art students at
Kalamazoo Institute of Arts
1948

Educator
Walden Baskerville
**First full-time African American male
teacher for Kalamazoo Public Schools**
1950

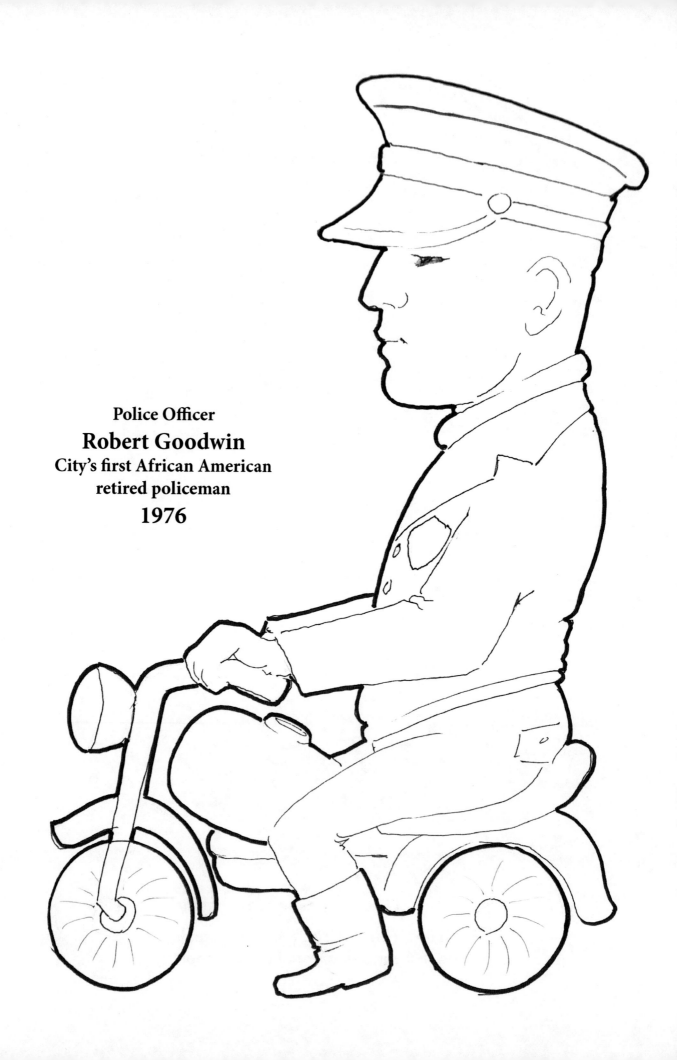

Police Officer
Robert Goodwin
City's first African American
retired policeman
1976

Fire Marshal
Dwight King, Sr.
First African American firefighter,
dispatcher and fire marshal in
Kalamazoo County
1954

Commissioner
Arthur Washington
City's first African American
commissioner
1959

Professor
Dr. Romeo Phillips
**First African American tenured professor at
Kalamazoo College**
1968

Mayor
Gilbert Bradley
City's first African American mayor
1971

Attorney
Leroy Densmore
**First African American assistant district attorney
in Kalamazoo County**

CITY OF KALAMAZOO

City Manager
Robert Bobb
Kalamazoo's first African American
city manager
1977

Music Producer
Narada Michael Walden
Kalamazoo's first Grammy-winning producer
1985

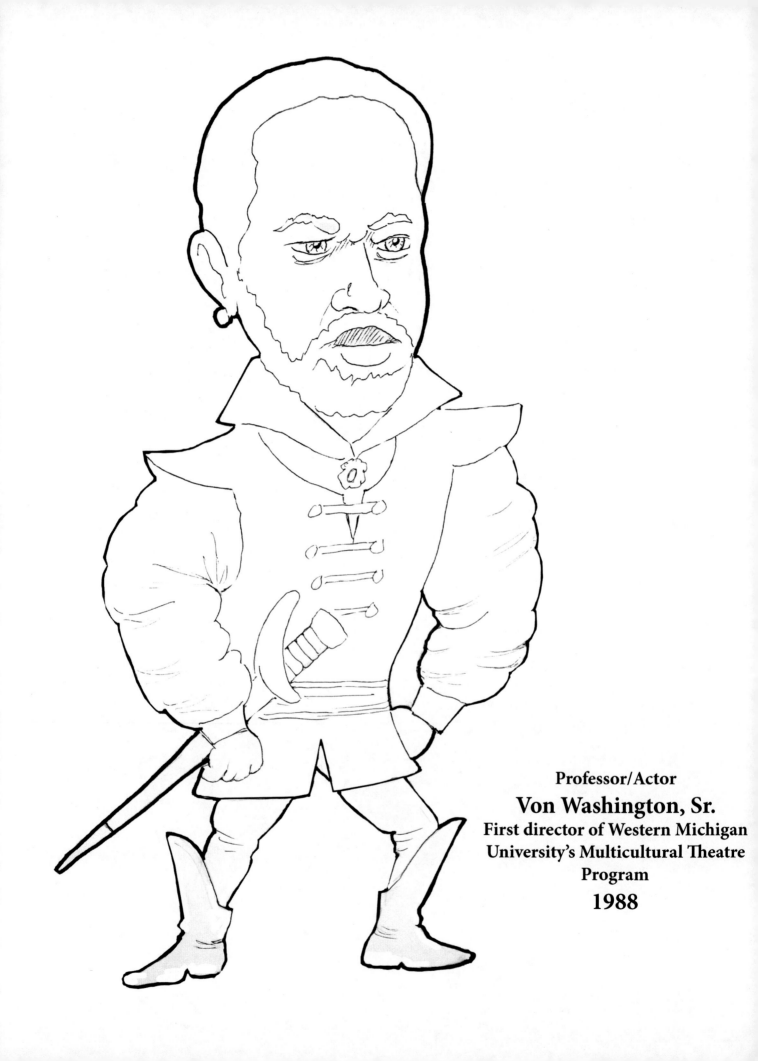

Professor/Actor
Von Washington, Sr.
First director of Western Michigan
University's Multicultural Theatre
Program
1988

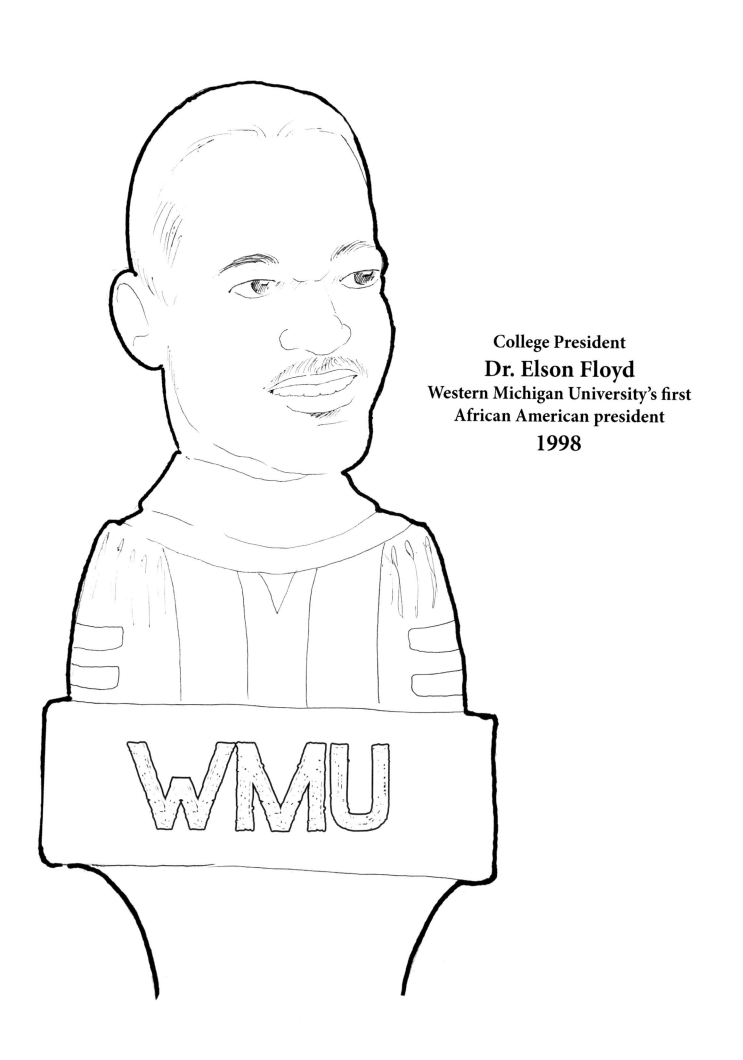

College President
Dr. Elson Floyd
Western Michigan University's first
African American president
1998

World Series Champion/Team Owner
Derek Jeter
Kalamazoo's first World Series champion
and first African American CEO
of a major league baseball team
2017

College President
Dr. L. Marshall Washington
First African American president of Kalamazoo Valley Community College
2018

Police Chief
Vernon Coakley
Kalamazoo Department of Public Safety's
First African American police chief
2020

What Do YOU Want to Become?
Draw a picture of you in the future.

My name is _____ .

I want to be a _____ .

African American Men of Kalamazoo

Use the clues to name the man who made history in Kalamazoo.

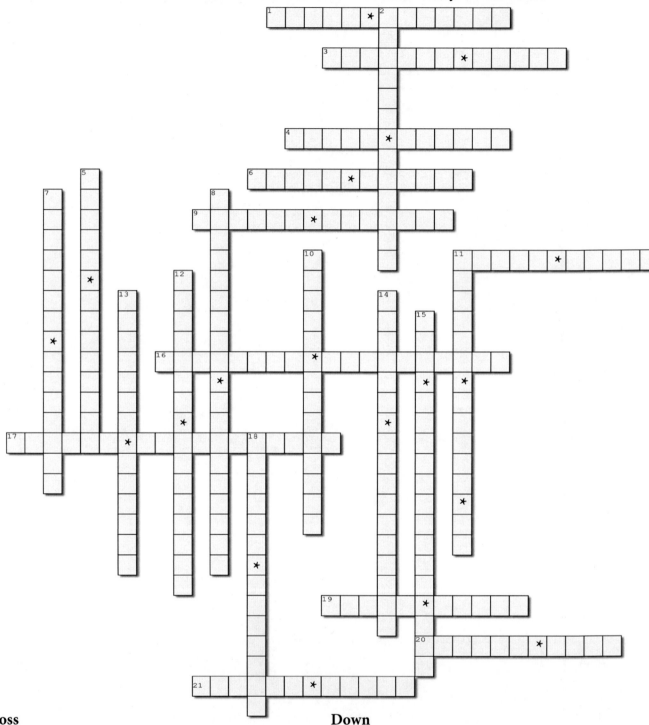

Across

1. WMU's first African American graduate
3. First African American lawyer and judge in Kalamazoo
4. First African American mail carrier
6. First African American settler of Kalamazoo County
9. Kalamazoo's first African American retired policeman
11. Kalamazoo's first World Series champion
16. KVCC's first African American president
17. First African American male teacher for KPS
19. First African American president of WMU
20. City's first African American city manager
21. First African American mason in Kalamazoo

Down

2. One of first African American art students at KIA
5. City's first African American assistant district attorney
7. Kalamazoo's first African American mayor
8. City's first African American surgeon
10. K-College's first African American tenured professor
11. City's first African American fire marshal
12. City's first African American justice of the peace
13. Kalamazoo's Grammy winning producer
14. City's first African American city commissioner
15. First director of WMU's Multicultural Theatre program
18. Kalamazoo's first African American police chief

African American Men of Kalamazoo
Find the names of the men who made Kalamazoo history!

W	R	U	I	X	E	V	O	N	W	A	S	H	I	N	G	T	O	N	Y
F	K	S	O	P	R	O	M	E	O	P	H	I	L	L	I	P	S	Z	V
W	A	L	L	A	C	E	S	T	A	F	F	O	R	D	B	K	I	U	F
Q	W	D	G	R	O	B	E	R	T	G	O	O	D	W	I	N	Q	Z	H
X	Q	N	F	R	A	N	K	W	I	L	S	O	N	N	L	I	U	M	V
C	L	E	R	O	Y	D	E	N	S	M	O	R	E	R	N	A	R	C	E
A	U	R	W	N	A	D	L	M	M	H	Q	D	X	U	V	L	O	D	I
R	P	L	Z	E	N	O	C	H	H	A	R	R	I	S	M	B	B	J	V
T	T	M	Y	X	S	N	Y	F	K	W	A	K	O	H	A	E	E	F	G
H	J	M	I	C	H	A	E	L	W	A	L	D	E	N	R	R	R	N	I
U	P	B	E	C	D	U	E	O	K	L	J	W	E	J	S	T	T	D	L
R	V	B	R	I	W	R	Z	I	Y	D	N	E	E	E	H	W	B	H	B
W	F	R	O	V	L	E	V	H	V	E	A	I	P	S	A	H	O	H	E
A	Q	I	F	S	Y	D	Z	D	T	N	I	Q	U	W	L	I	B	T	R
S	T	Z	K	N	S	E	J	H	O	B	W	F	D	T	L	T	B	Q	T
H	I	G	T	J	A	R	H	G	S	A	F	G	E	U	W	E	H	V	B
I	C	C	O	R	N	E	L	I	U	S	A	L	E	X	A	N	D	E	R
N	M	N	H	I	J	K	N	I	T	K	J	D	D	Z	S	X	G	R	A
G	O	C	J	C	U	J	C	S	Q	E	P	W	E	G	H	M	O	N	D
T	S	V	U	Y	H	E	P	L	X	R	R	G	I	E	I	F	S	O	L
O	C	Q	K	W	B	T	R	X	L	V	Q	A	I	I	N	V	A	N	E
N	A	K	W	M	M	E	W	B	F	I	D	U	Y	J	G	U	B	C	Y
B	R	I	W	R	O	R	C	D	I	L	R	M	D	Y	T	Q	M	O	N
J	M	Z	U	T	P	O	O	Y	D	L	F	C	P	V	O	I	A	A	H
X	I	H	C	R	V	E	N	L	T	E	B	Y	D	K	N	F	M	K	N
W	T	D	W	I	G	H	T	K	I	N	G	A	M	T	C	E	O	L	S
W	C	A	V	E	E	U	I	M	U	R	P	H	Y	D	A	R	D	E	N
K	H	O	O	E	L	S	O	N	F	L	O	Y	D	K	S	I	D	Y	I
C	E	W	V	H	C	H	A	R	L	E	S	P	R	A	T	T	Y	R	U
O	M	P	Y	Q	E	J	B	I	O	E	H	L	W	R	C	K	P	J	G

Enoch Harris	Murphy Darden	Gilbert Bradley	Leroy Densmore
Charles Pratt	Arthur Washington	Wallace Stafford	Von Washington
Robert Bobb	Michael Walden	Albert White	Elson Floyd
Dwight King	Walden Baskerville	Marshall Washington	Romeo Phillips
Robert Goodwin	Frank Wilson	Oscar Mitchem	Cornelius Alexander
Vernon Coakley	Derek Jeter		

Unscramble the words below.

1. NACMOIPEL   A PERSON WHO PROTECTS AND SERVES THE COMMUNITY

2. OOCDRT   SOMEONE WHO HELPS HEAL OTHERS

3. GUJDE   A PERSON WHO HEARS CASES IN COURT

4. MIFAERN   A PERSON WHO FIGHTS FIRES

5. YRAOM   SOMEONE ELECTED TO LEAD A CITY

6. BSEAALBL   SOMETHING HIT BY A BAT

7. ECHTRAE   THE PERSON WHO HELPS OTHERS LEARN

8. RPOFEOSRS   A COLLEGE TEACHER

9. AMLI   SOMETHING DELIVERED TO A HOME

10. ELRTETS   A PERSON WHO MAKES A NEW PLACE THEIR HOME

Crossword Answer

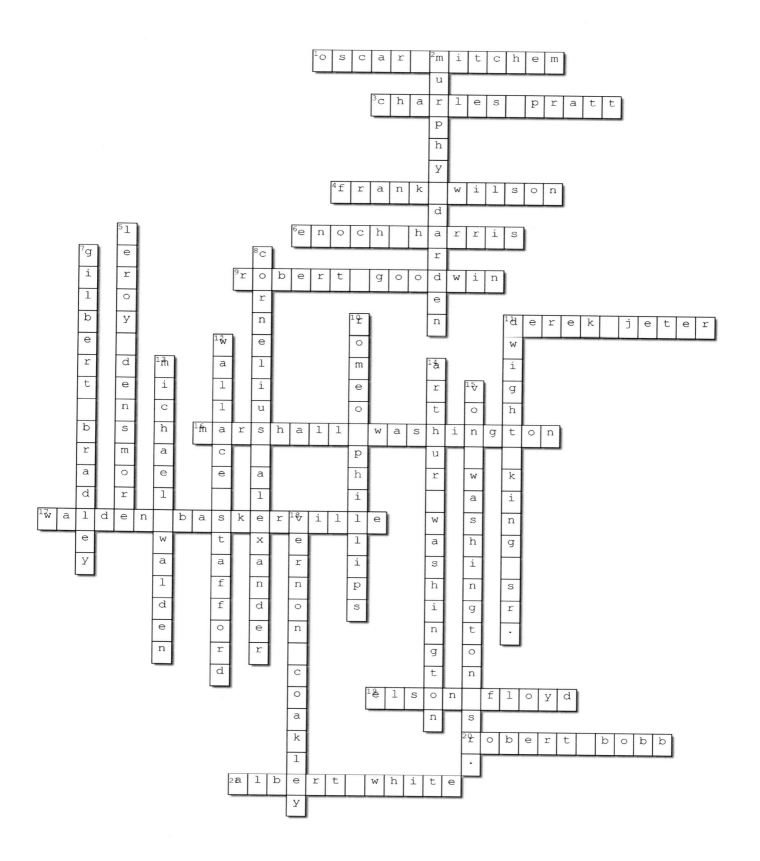

Word Search Answers

```
W R U I X E V O N W A S H I N G T O N Y
F K S O P R O M E O P H I L L I P S Z V
W A L L A C E S T A F F O R D B K I U F
Q W D G R O B E R T G O O D W I N Q Z H
X Q N F R A N K W I L S O N N L I U M V
C L E R O Y D E N S M O R E R N A R C E
A U R W N A D L M M H Q D X U V L O D I
R P L Z E N O C H H A R R I S M B B J V
T T M Y X S N Y F K W A K O H A E E F G
H J M I C H A E L W A L D E N R R R N I
U P B E C D U E O K L J W E J S T T D L
R V B R I W R Z I Y D N E E E E H B H B
W F R O V L E V H V E A I P S A H O H E
A Q I F S Y D Z D T N I Q U W L I B T R
S T Z K N S E J H O B W F D T L T B Q T
H I G T J A R H G S A F G E U W E H V B
I C C O R N E L I U S A L E X A N D E R
N M N H I J K N I T K J D D Z S X G R A
G O C J C U J C S Q E P W E G H M O N D
T S V U Y H E P L X R R G I E I F S O L
O C Q K W B T R X L V Q A I I N V A N E
N A K W M M E W B F I D U Y J G U B C Y
B R I W R O R C D I L R M D Y T Q M O N
J M Z U T P O O Y D L F C P V O I A A H
X I H C R V E N L T E B Y D K N F M K N
W T D W I G H T K I N G A M T C E O L S
W C A V E E U I M U R P H Y D A R D E N
K H O O E L S O N F L O Y D K S I D Y I
C E W V H C H A R L E S P R A T T Y R U
O M P Y Q E J B I O E H L W R C K P J G
```

Unscramble Answers

#	Scrambled	Answer	Clue
1.	NACMOIPEL	POLICEMAN	A PERSON WHO PROTECTS AND SERVES THE COMMUNITY
2.	OOCDRT	DOCTOR	SOMEONE WHO HELPS HEAL OTHERS
3.	GUJDE	JUDGE	A PERSON WHO HEARS CASES IN COURT
4.	MIFAERN	FIREMAN	A PERSON WHO FIGHTS FIRES
5.	YRAOM	MAYOR	SOMEONE ELECTED TO LEAD A CITY
6.	BSEAALBL	BASEBALL	SOMETHING HIT BY A BAT
7.	ECHTRAE	TEACHER	THE PERSON WHO HELPS OTHERS LEARN
8.	RPOFEOSRS	PROFESSOR	A COLLEGE TEACHER
9.	AMLI	MAIL	SOMETHING DELIVERED TO A HOME
10.	ELRTETS	SETTLER	A PERSON WHO MAKES A NEW PLACE THEIR HOME

African American Men First of Kalamazoo

Kalamazoo, Michigan, is a small town between Detroit and Chicago. Its location provided a hometown atmosphere in close proximity to big-city experiences. The men who lived in the community brought talents, drive, and determination to make a difference in the lives of their families. Their trials and triumphs led them to become some of our city's most valued, yet often unsung, history makers.

1830- Enoch Harris and his wife Deborah moved to what is now Oshtemo Township in 1830. They became the first African American settlers in Kalamazoo County and went on to own more than 200 acres of land that included the county's first apple orchard.
(Source: Tarvarious Haywood, *News Channel 3 WWMT*, "First African Americans to settle in Kalamazoo County," February 21, 2020.)

1870s- Albert White helped build several important buildings in Kalamazoo, including the original Borgess Hospital, East Hall at Western Michigan University, and the third Kalamazoo Central High School. He was born in Canton, Indiana, and came to Kalamazoo in the 1870s at the age of 15. By age 25 his was the first local African American construction contracting business to employ all races.
(Source: *https://www.kpl.gov/local-history/kalamazoo-history/black-history/albert-white/*, "Albert White: African American Builder Broke Racial Barriers.")

1891- Frank Wilson was born in Kalamazoo in 1865. He worked as a journeyman painter and then for a grocery store before becoming a substitute mail carrier. In 1891 he was appointed a regular mail carrier in Kalamazoo and held one of the most important routes in the city.
(Source: Rev. John Davis, Publisher, *Afro-American Journal and Directory,* 1894, Kalamazoo Public Library.)

1894- Wallace Stafford completed high school in Kalamazoo in 1890. He worked as a law clerk for local attorneys and in 1894 became the second African American in the city nominated to run for a local office. Wallace won his race and became the city's first African American justice of the peace.
(Source: Rev. John Davis, Publisher, Afro-American Journal and Directory, 1894, Kalamazoo Public Library.)

1917- Oscar Mitchem became the first African American graduate of Western State Normal School, later to be named Western Michigan University. During his time at the college he also was the first African American member of the marching band.
(Source: *https://www.timetoast.com/Paving the Way.*)

1931- Cornelius Alexander grew up in Chattanooga, Tennessee, and after high school went on to graduate from Fisk University in 1923. In 1929, Cornelius graduated from Rush Medical College at the of University of Chicago, coming to Kalamazoo in 1931 to open his own medical practice. He became an active member of the community and served as the city's first African American doctor and surgeon for more than 50 years.
(Source: *Western News*, "Book published by Department of History chronicles life of Alexander," January 4, 1996.)

1935- Charles Pratt graduated from Kalamazoo Central High School in 1928. He left Kalamazoo to attend Howard University, where he earned his law degree in 1935. He returned home and became the city's first African American to start his own law practice. In 1968 he was elected Michigan's Eighth District Judge, making him the first African American judge in Kalamazoo.
(Source: *Kalamazoo College Honorary Doctorate Ceremony,* Pratt-Degree Citation, 1981.)

1948- Murphy Darden moved to Kalamazoo from Aberdeen, Mississippi, in 1948 with his wife, Manassa, and his twin brother, Irvin. In 1948 the brothers became the first African American men to take classes at the now Kalamazoo Institute of Arts. In 2018 Darden earned the State History Award from the Historical Society of Michigan for his cowboy and African American history collection.
(Source: Jennifer Clark, *Encore Magazine*, "Wrangling Black History: Murphy Darden lassos the past," February 2019.)

1950- Walden Baskerville came to Kalamazoo in 1950 and worked at the Douglass Community Center for four years. He later became the first full-time African American teacher for Kalamazoo Public Schools. He worked as a shop teacher at Lincoln Junior High and as a counselor before becoming a professor at Western Michigan University.
(Source: *Dr. Cornelius Allen Alexander interview tapes*, Kalamazoo Public Library Miller Local History Room.)

1951- Robert Goodwin joined the Kalamazoo Department of Public Safety in 1951 as a police officer. He worked with the department until 1976 when he made history as the first African American to retire from that department in Kalamazoo.
(Source: Steve VanBergen, *FOX17*, "First black officer who retired from Kalamazoo gets posthumous promotion," February 1, 2016.)

1954- Dwight King, Sr., graduated from Kalamazoo Central High School in 1948 and joined the Air Force. He returned home and in 1954 became the city's first African American firefighter and fire dispatcher. Before he retired in 1994, he also would become the city's first African American fire marshal.
(Source: *https://www.betzlerlifestory.com/obituaries/dwight-king*)

1959- Arthur Washington was elected to the Kalamazoo City Commission in 1959. He served in that role until 1966 while also being a leader for civil rights. He served as president of the local NAACP and was honored by various organizations for his work as a public servant. In 2003, the city named its police department and court building the City of Kalamazoo Arthur Washington Jr Crosstown Center.
(Source: *Harperfuneral.com/arthurwashington*.)

1968- Romeo Phillips, Ph.D., came to Kalamazoo in 1968 to serve as the first tenured African American professor at Kalamazoo College. His presence at the college was instrumental in race relations with students of color and earned him a Fulbright Scholarship to teach in Africa. His service to the communities of Kalamazoo and Portage included roles as president of the local NAACP and Portage City Council. Dr. Phillips' musical talents led him to serve as a vocal coach for Motown artists and for diverse musical ensembles.
(Source: Sharekazoo.org/staff-and-board.)

1971- Gilbert Bradley, a former director of the Douglass Community Center, joined the Kalamazoo City Commission in 1969 as vice-mayor. Nineteen candidates ran for the city commission in 1971. Bradley earned the most votes that year to earn the title as the city's first African American mayor.
(Source: Dave Benson, *WKFR 103.3*, "First Black Kalamazoo Mayor Gil Bradley Dies at 77," May 29, 2018.)

1973- Leroy Densmore moved from Inkster, Michigan, to Kalamazoo to study theater at Western Michigan University. He decided to pursue law and earned a juris doctorate from Wayne State University in 1973. He passed the bar and became the first African American assistant district attorney in Kalamazoo County.
(Source: *https://www.celestis.com/participants-testimonials/leroy-evins-densmore-jr/*)

1977- Robert Bobb made history as the longest-serving African American city manager in the nation. That history began in 1977 when he was elected the first African American city manager in Kalamazoo. He later became a city manager in such places as Oakland, California, Richmond, Virginia, Santa Ana, California, and as a Homeland Security Advisor in Washington, D.C., among many other government-appointed leadership roles across the country.
(Source: *Michigan Municipal League, mml.org,* "Robert Bobb to Speak at Michigan Municipal League Convention," August 9. 2010.)

1985- Narada Michael Walden was born in Kalamazoo in 1956 and graduated from Plainwell High School. After three semesters studying music at Western Michigan University, he left to chase his dream as a musician. He won his first of three Grammy Awards in 1985 for Best R&B Song as co-writer of "Freeway of Love," performed by Aretha Franklin, and has written hits for those such as Whitney Houston, Stevie Wonder, and Ray Charles.
(Source: Mark Wedel, *Kalamazoo Gazette,* "Kalamazoo still feels like home for drummer and Grammy winning producer Narada Michael Walden," August 6, 2012.)

1988- Von Washington, Sr., served as the first director of Western Michigan University's Multicultural Theatre program. His passion for theater and history led him to form the award-winning Washington Productions with his family. Their plays have been performed for thousands of all ages for stage and radio.
(Source: Sonya Bernard-Hollins, *Kalamazoo Gazette,* "Von Washington winds down his career," April 4, 2010.)

1998- Elson Floyd, Ph.D., served as the sixth president and first African American president of Western Michigan University. He served WMU from 1998 to 2003 and became the first African American president of Washington State University in 2007.
(Source: *WMU News,* "Former President Elson Floyd dies in Washington," June 20, 2015.)

2017- Derek Jeter graduated from Kalamazoo Central High School and went on to make history in major league baseball. After high school, he was signed to a minor league baseball team and eventually to the New York Yankees, where he won five World Series championships. His No. 2 jersey was retired in 2017 when he left the field to lead the Jeter Publishing imprint of Simon & Schuster and become part-owner of the Miami Marlins. He is the first African American to serve as CEO of a major league team.
(Source: *https://mlb.com/turn-2-foundation/derek-jeter/bio.*)

2018- Marshall Washington, Ph.D., became the third president and first African American president of Kalamazoo Valley Community College in 2018. He previously served as president and vice president at colleges in West Virginia, Pennsylvania, and Michigan.
(*KV Focus*, Kalamazoo Valley Community College, October 2018.)

2020- Vernon Coakley became the first African American police chief for the Kalamazoo Department of Public Safety in 2020. Before coming to Kalamazoo in 1993, he served in the Detroit Police Department. He has academic degrees from Western Michigan and Ferris State universities and attended the Federal Bureau of Investigation National Academy.
(Source: Brad Devereaux, *MLIVE.com,* "Vernon Coakley sworn in as Kalamazoo Public Safety chief," October 1, 2020.)

For permission requests, write to the publisher, addressed "Attention: Permissions Coordinator,"
Season Press LLC/Community Voices
P.O. Box 51042
Kalamazoo, MI 49001

Ordering Information:
Quantity sales. Special discounts are available on quantity purchases by non-profit organizations, corporations, and others. For details, contact the publisher at the address above.

Published in collaboration with Fortitude Graphic Design & Printing and Season Press LLC
Design and Layout by Sean Hollins
Illustrations by Jerome Washington
Edited by Maggie Zahrai

This is a multimedia history project created by the Merze Tate Explorers

To learn more about this Your Turn project visit:
https://www.merzetate.org

Publisher's Cataloging-in-Publication data
Hollins, Sonya.
Your Turn: African American Men Firsts of Kalamazoo
p. cm.
ISBN 978-1-7353600-8-9
Library of Congress Control
Number: 2021902277

1. African American History—Juvenile Literature. 2. Men in History—Kalamazoo, Michigan.

A Community Voices Imprint
First Edition
10 9 8 7 6 5 4 3 2 1
Printed in the United States of America

Made in the USA
Coppell, TX
07 June 2023